Steck-Vaughn

Think-Alongs™

Comprehending As You Read

Level A

Program Authors

Senior Author
Roger Farr

Co-Authors
Jennifer Conner
Elizabeth Haydel
Bruce Tone
Beth Greene
Tanja Bisesi
Cheryl Gilliland

STECK-VAUGHN
ELEMENTARY · SECONDARY · ADULT · LIBRARY

A Harcourt Classroom Education Company

www.steck-vaughn.com

Acknowledgments

Editorial Director	Diane Schnell
Project Editor	Anne Souby
Associate Director of Design	Cynthia Ellis
Design Manager	Ted Krause
Production and Design	Julia Miracle-Hagaman
Photo Editor	Claudette Landry
Product Manager	Patricia Colacino
Cover Design	Ted Krause
Cover Sculpture	Lonnie Springer
Cover Production	Alan Klemp

Think-Alongs™ is a trademark of Steck-Vaughn Company.

ISBN 0-7398-0083-3

6 7 8 9 PO 03 02

Contents

Drawing Pictures
That Tell the Story

Read the story below.

A big dog ran into the classroom.

He bumped the fish bowl.

It crashed to the floor.

He bumped the bookcase.

Down came a pile of books.

"Whose dog is this?" asked the teacher.

The dog ran to Tony's desk.

He jumped in his lap.

"It's my dog," Tony said.

"I'll take him home."

**Draw a picture
of the story.
Write about it.**

So Can I

By Margery Facklam

This story is about animals and what they do.
What can you do that animals can do?

A fish can swim.
So can I.

6

A monkey can swing.

So can I.

A dog can dig.

So can I.

A horse can run.

So can I.

A rabbit can hop.

So can I.

A frog can jump.

So can I.

A squirrel can climb.

So can I.

A bear can hug.

So can I.

A bird can fly.
So can I.
But I need some help!

Time to Write!

Draw a picture about the story.
Write about your picture.

_____

_____

15

There Is a Town

By Gail Herman

Let's Read

This story tells about a room—in a house—on a street—in a town. What happens in the room in the house?

There is a town.
And in this town,
there is a street.

And on this street,
there is a house.
And in this house,
there is a room.
And in this room,
there is a box.

And in this box,
there is a house.
And in this house,
there is a room.
And in this room,
there is a box.

Time to Write!

What did you find out about bears?
Draw a picture.
Write about your picture.

33

What Happened to You

Have you ever gone shopping?
Read the story below.

The Three Bears went shopping.

Baby Bear got black boots like Papa Bear's.

Mama Bear got a new pot for oatmeal.

Papa Bear said, "I need a new hat to keep the sun out of my eyes."

He bought a hat made out of straw.

Baby Bear said, "Let's buy something for Grandma Bear."

They looked in all the stores.

"It's not easy to find something for Grandma Bear," said Baby Bear.

Think about a
time you went
shopping.
Draw a picture.
Write about it.

_____

My Sister Is My Friend

By Hannah Markley

Let's Read

This story is about a little boy and his big sister.
She helps him.
How do older people help you?

My sister finds my socks.

My sister finds my shoes.

My sister finds my book.

My sister finds my coat.

My sister finds my snake.

I'm glad my sister is my friend.

Time to Write!

Who helps you?
Draw a picture.
Write about your picture.

41

All Kinds of Wheels

By Stephanie Handwerker

Let's Read

**This story is about things that have wheels.
What do you ride that has wheels?**

I have one large wheel.
You can ride me at the fair.

I have two wheels.
You can ride me anywhere.

I have three wheels.
I fly down to the ground.

I have four wheels.
Pull me to turn around.

I have five wheels.
Count my spare tire, too.

I have many wheels.
The sound I make is choo-choo.

Here are wheels of every kind.
How many wheels can you find?

Time to Write!

What can you ride that has wheels?
Draw a picture.
Write about your picture.

Sam's Seasons

By Christine Price

This story is about a boy named Sam.
He is looking for his boots.
Have you ever looked for something?

Sam, where are your boots?

Mom, do I have to find them today?

I don't remember where I left them.

50

Sam, please find your boots.

Last spring, I wore them in the rain.
I splashed in the water puddles.

Sam, please find your boots.

Last summer, I wore them to the beach.
I filled them with sand to make a castle.

Sam, please find
your boots.

Last autumn, I wore them in the leaves.
I raked the leaves into a pile and
jumped in.

Sam, please find
your boots.

Last winter, I wore them in the snow.
I used them to help stop my sled.

Sam, please find your boots.
They must be somewhere in here.
I know I wore them all four seasons.

But Sam, where are your boots NOW?

I found them!

But look, Mom, now my boots are too small.

Time to Write!

Have you ever lost something?

Draw a picture.

Write about your picture.

_____

_____

Thinking Along on Tests

Read the stories.

Answer the questions.

Where will the robin live?

The robin sees a fat worm.

Hop … hop … hop … hop.

"The robin needs a place to live,"
the girl says.
"After I eat," the robin says.
Hop … hop … hop … hop.

The girl has a house for the robin.

"Here is your house, Robin," she says.

But the robin doesn't come to it.

Hop … hop … hop … hop.

A little bird goes flying by.
"Oh, hurry, Robin!" the girl says.
"Another bird will get your house."
The robin does not seem to care.
Hop … hop … hop … hop.

"I have to eat first," Robin says.
"Thank you just the same.
Let the little bird have the house.
I will build my nest in a tree.
That would be the best for me."
Hop … hop … hop … hop.

Sample: Where is the robin?

◯   ◯   ◯

in the house   in the nest   on the ground

1. What does the girl have for the robin?

○

a house

○

a nest

○

a friend

---

2. Who will live in the birdhouse?

○

the robin

○

the little bird

○

the girl

---

3. What does the robin want to do first?

○

fly

○

build a nest

○

eat

---

4. Where will the robin live?

○

in the house

○

in a nest

○

on the ground

5. What does the robin do all through the story?

Draw a picture. Write about your picture.

What happened to the castle?

Tillie and Willie went down to the sea.

They saw Sarah sitting in the sand.

Her dog Dingo barked at them.

Let's make a castle!" Sarah said.

Willie played in the waves.

"Let's all swim!" he cried.

"Come up here, Willie," Tillie called.

"Come and help us with the castle."

They all made a castle.

It was big and beautiful.

But the waves washed up close to it.

"The waves have followed Willie,"

Sarah said.

Soon the waves washed away the castle.

Dingo hid his head.

"How sad!" Sarah cried.

"Oh, no," Tillie said.

"Tomorrow we'll make a new one!"

6. Who was sitting in the sand?

○
Tillie

○
Willie

○
Sarah

7. What did Sarah want to do?

○
play in
the waves

○
make
a castle

○
go
swimming

8. What happened to the castle?

○
It washed away.

○
Dingo ran over it.

○
It stayed.

9. How does Sarah feel at the end of the story?

○
happy

○
sad

○
angry

10. What did the children make?

Draw a picture. Write about your picture.

(blank box for drawing)

(blank writing line)

What does Charlie do?

My cat Charlie
   is very, very old.
He's the oldest cat you'll see.

My cat Charlie
   is very, very orange.
He's orange as orange can be.

My cat Charlie
   sleeps all day long.
That's just what old cats do.

My cat Charlie
   goes out at night.
But he sleeps when he's out there, too.

My cat Charlie
    has yellow eyes.
At least I think he does.
He used to be a lively cat.
Well, maybe Charlie was.

My cat Charlie
    is very, very old.
He doesn't fight or play.

My cat Charlie
    is very, very orange.
And he sleeps both night and day.

11. What color is Charlie?

○ ○ ○

black white orange

---

12. What does Charlie do all day?

○ ○ ○

plays sleeps eats

---

13. How old is Charlie?

○ ○ ○

just a kitten not very old very, very old

---

14. Why can't we be sure what color Charlie's eyes are?

○ ○ ○

He wears
sunglasses. They are
always shut. They
change colors.

15. What does Charlie do outdoors at night?
Draw a picture. Write about your picture.

The Main Idea of the Story

Read the story below.
Think about the main idea of the story.

Annie loves her cat, Tabby.

Every morning she feeds her.

Annie eats breakfast.

Tabby eats, too.

Annie goes to school.

Tabby can not go to school.

Tabby waits for Annie at home.

After school, Tabby and Annie play.

At night, Tabby sleeps on Annie's bed.

"Good night, Tabby," Annie says.

"Meow," Tabby says.

What is this story mainly about?

Draw a picture.

This story made me think that pets are fun!

Write about your picture.

_____

Read and Think

- Read the stories.
- Stop at each box. Answer the question.
- Think about the main idea.

Soccer Game!

By Grace Maccarone

Let's Read

This story is about playing soccer. The blue team tells the story. Read the story to find out how to play soccer and who wins the game.

We start the game.
We're ready.
We aim.
We pass.

Yin-May read the letter.

"Emma is my best friend," she said.

"I wonder what the string is for."

"I don't know," said Yin-May's mom.

She found a very long piece of string
for Yin-May.

At six o'clock Yin-May
looked out of her window.
"What a surprise," she said.
She saw all her friends
who had been at Emma's party.
They had balloons and party hats.
They clapped their hands and waved
when they saw Yin-May at the window.

2 Draw a picture of Yin-May's friends.

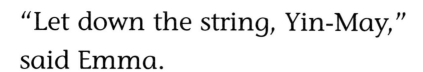

"Let down the string, Yin-May,"
said Emma.
"But keep one end in your hand."
So Yin-May let down the string and
Emma tied the end to a basket.
Then all her friends put a present
for Yin-May in the basket.

There were balloons and candy and cards and a big piece of birthday cake from Emma.

"You are a good friend," said Yin-May.

"Now I can join in the party, too."

 3 Draw a picture of Yin-May at the end of the story.

Time to Write!

Think of a party you went to. Draw a picture of you and your friends at a party.

Write about your picture.
Where was the party?

_____

_____

Pet Day

By Lois Bick

This story is about Pet Day. Read the story to find out what pets the students bring to school on Pet Day.

On Pet Day, all the kids take their pets to school. Every pet wins a prize.

1 What pet would you like to bring? Draw a picture. Write about it.

Last year on Pet Day,
Jerome's dog won a prize.
The dog is very big.

Marcy's snake won a prize.
The snake is very long.

Juan's bird won a prize.
The bird is very loud.
Cassie's rabbit won
a prize, too.
The rabbit has pretty eyes.
But I didn't win anything
because I don't have a pet.

2 How does the girl telling the story feel?
Draw a picture. Write about it.

This year I had an idea.
I went outside by the front steps,
and I started to hunt.

Then I found something special
to take to school.

I knew that my pets would win
a prize this year.

Jerome brought his mouse.
He chased it most of the day.
Marcy carried her guinea pig.
She let everyone hold it.

Juan held his turtle.
He couldn't get it to
come out of its shell.

Cassie walked in with her monkey.
She trained it to do tricks.

And do you know what?
My pets won a prize, too.
And everyone loved catching
my grasshoppers.

3 Draw a picture of the classroom on Pet Day. Write about Pet Day.

Think of a pet you have or a pet you would like to have.

Draw a picture of you and a pet.

Write about your picture.
What prize would your pet win on Pet Day?

_____

_____

Thinking About

What Might Happen Next

Read the story below.

What do you think will happen?

A caterpillar sat in the warm sun.

A bee flew by.

"You can fly," said the caterpillar.

The caterpillar tried to fly, but he could not.

He felt very sad.

The caterpillar fell asleep.

He slept for a long time.

When he woke up, he was surprised.

He had large wings with bright colors.

He could fly!

Now he was a butterfly.

And he was happy.

Check what you thought would happen in the story.

I thought the caterpillar would become a butterfly.

☐ The caterpillar would not be able to fly.

☐ The caterpillar would fall asleep.

☐ The caterpillar would be happy.

What else did you think about?

_____

_____

_____

_____

Read and Think

- Read the stories.
- Stop at each box. Answer the question.
- Think about what might happen next.

My Boat

By Kay Davies and Wendy Oldfield

This story is about different boats.
Read the story to find out what the
different boats can do.

Look at all these boats!
How many can you see?
What colors and shapes are they?

My boat is long and red.
My boat is flat at one end
and pointed at the other end.

My boat floats on water.
It does not let water in.

If I make waves, my boat moves
away from me.

What will happen if I put some marbles in my boat?

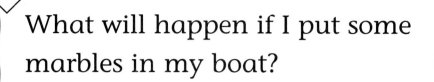

1 What do you think will happen if the boy puts marbles in the boat?

If the marbles are all at one end of my boat —it sinks!

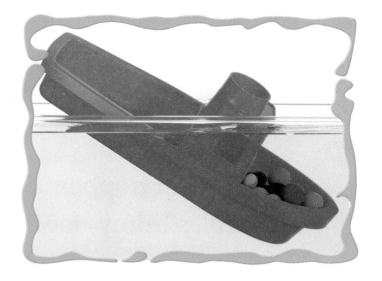

With marbles at both ends, my boat floats low in the water.

If I add too many marbles . . . !

 2 What do you think will happen if he adds more marbles?

Tom is making
a paper boat.

It floats on the water.
What happens when
Tom's boat soaks
up the water?

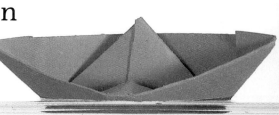

3 What do you think will happen when
Tom's boat soaks up the water?

I'm making
clay boats.
Do you think
they will float?

My clay boat has
a mast and a sail.
When we blow on
the sail, my boat
moves in the
water.

 4   What else could you use to make a boat?

I have made a wooden boat.
With a drop of dishwashing
liquid, my boat moves
on its own.

Under Polly's wooden
boat, there is a keel.
It's hard to pull
Polly's boat over.
If I tip it sideways,
it swings back up again.

We are having a race with our boats.

What types of boats
can you make?

5 What kind of boat would you want to make?

Time to Write!

This story tells about different kinds of boats.

If you had a boat, what kind would you like to have?

Prewriting

● First, fill out the chart below.

Kinds of Boats	What I like about them	What I don't like about them
Paper boats		
Clay boats		
Wooden boats		

Writing

Now, use another sheet of paper. Write about the kind of boat you would like to have.

My New Boy

By Joan Phillips

Let's Read

This story is about a puppy who gets a new home with a little boy. Read the story to find out what the puppy does with his new boy.

I am a little black puppy.
I live in a pet store.

Soon I will have a kid of my own.
Many kids come.

1 What do you think the kids will do with the puppy?

This one pulls my tail.

This one kisses too much.
They are not for me.

Here is another kid.

He says hello.

He pats my head.

Woof! Woof!

This is the boy for me!

My new boy takes me home.

I start taking care of my boy right away.

2 How do you think the puppy will take care of the boy?

I help him eat dinner.

I keep him clean.

I teach him to play tug of war.

I teach him to throw a ball to me.

I show my boy tricks.

I sit up.

I roll over.

I teach my boy to give

me a bone every time I do a trick.

My boy is not good at everything.

 3 What do you think the puppy can do better than the boy?

He can not dig very fast.

He can not scratch
his ears with his foot.

He can not hide under the bed.

My boy can not run as fast as I can.

I run and run.

Oh, no!

I do not see my boy.

Is he lost?

 4 What do you think the puppy will do?

I look behind a tree.
I look on the rocks.
I do not see my boy.

117

Is he on the swing?
No.
Is he on the slide?
No.
I do not see my
boy anywhere.

Eric runs off in a dash.
He hides behind the neighbor's trash.

"I'll find you!" Marco gives a shout.
"Oh, no, you won't!" Suzanne cries out.

Marco says, "I think that tree
Just talked. In fact, it yelled at me!"

He tags Suzanne on the other side.
"You're 'It'," he says. "Now I can hide."

Sample: Where was Tracy hiding?

behind a tree   behind the trash   behind a wall

1. Who was "It" when the game began?

○
Suzanne

○
Tracy

○
Marco

2. Who is "It" when the story ends?

○
Marco

○
Suzanne

○
Eric

3. Why did Marco find Suzanne?

○
She talked.

○
She ran away.

○
She is tall.

4. How many players are "It" at one time?

○
one

○
two

○
three

5. Where did Eric hide?

Draw a picture. Write about your picture.

What color is the sky?

Paulo was making a picture.

He made a green tree.

Then he drew a red barn.

He wanted to make his sky.

Bradley had Paulo's blue crayon.

"That's my crayon," Paulo said.

Nina was drawing her family.

"He's right," she said.

"That is Paulo's crayon."

"I need the crayon," Bradley said.

"It's blue.

I am making the sky on my picture."

"Let Bradley finish his sky," Nina said.

"He won't use all of the blue crayon."

"Look!" Bradley said.
"I have a beautiful blue sky.
But Paulo's sky is yellow!"
"I made a sunny day," Paulo said.
"It is sunny because I get to play with
two good friends."

6. Who makes a blue sky?

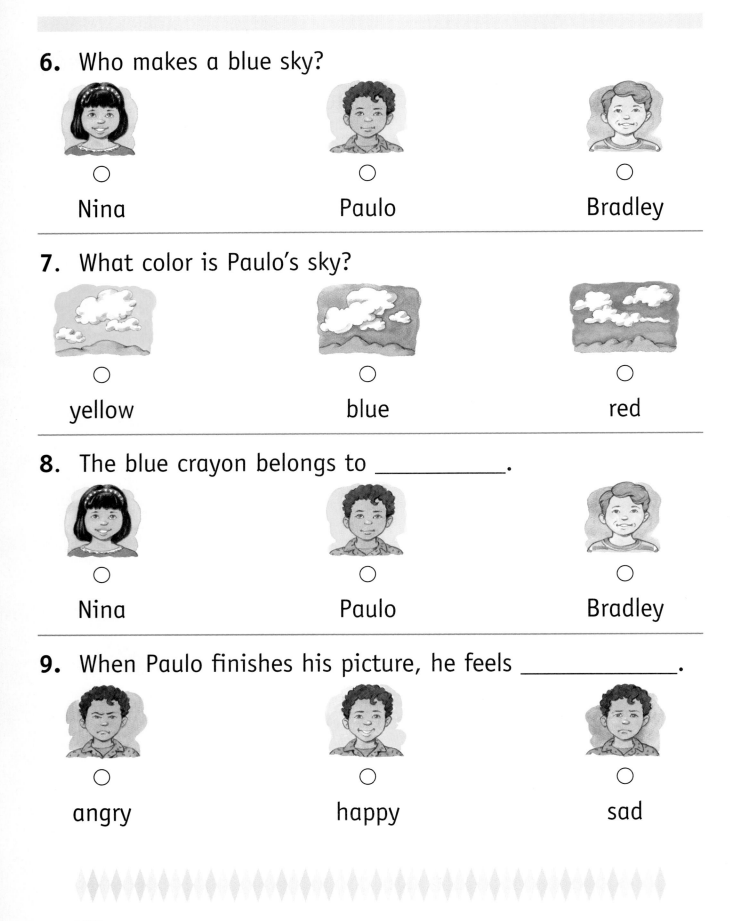

○ Nina   ○ Paulo   ○ Bradley

7. What color is Paulo's sky?

○ yellow   ○ blue   ○ red

8. The blue crayon belongs to _____.

○ Nina   ○ Paulo   ○ Bradley

9. When Paulo finishes his picture, he feels _____.

○ angry   ○ happy   ○ sad

10. What was Nina drawing?

Draw a picture. Write about your picture.

How fast can Maria run?

It was a windy day.

The children were playing in the yard.

"I can run very fast!" Maria cried.

"I can run faster than the wind!"

"Oh, sure you can," Kevin said.

He made a silly face.

"I can show you!" Maria said.

"Oh, come on!" Matt said.

"I want to go to the park."

"Just watch me!" Maria cried.

She ran into the house.

Maria looked out a window.

"Is it still windy out there?" she asked.

"Yes," Matt said.

"Well, there's no wind in here," she said.

"She beat the wind inside," Kevin said.

Maria stuck her head out the window.

The wind blew her hair all around.

"Oh, boy!" Matt said.

"The wind does not like losing."

11. Who tries to run faster than the wind?

○
Maria

○
Matt

○
Kevin

---

12. Where does Maria go?

○
to the park

○
in the yard

○
into the house

---

13. There is no wind in the _____.

○
yard

○
house

○
park

---

14. Matt thinks that the wind is _____.

○
sad

○
happy

○
angry

15. Where did Matt want to go?

Draw a picture. Write about your picture.

Acknowledgments

Grateful acknowledgment is made to the following authors and publishers for the use of copyrighted materials. Every effort has been made to obtain permission to use previously published material. Any errors or omissions are unintentional.

All Kinds of Wheels by Stephanie Handwerker. Copyright © 1997 by Steck-Vaughn Company.

Bears, Bears, and More Bears by Jackie Morris. Copyright © 1995. Reprinted by arrangement with Barron's Educational Series, Inc., Hauppage, New York.

Little Red and the Wolf by Gare Thompson. Copyright © 1997 by Steck-Vaughn Company.

My Boat by Kay Davies and Wendy Oldfield (Gareth Stevens, Inc.). By permission of Gareth Stevens, Inc. Copyright © A&C Black (Publishers) Ltd.

My New Boy by Joan Phillips. Text copyright © 1986 by Joan Phillips. Illustrations copyright © 1986 by Lynn Munsinger. Reprinted by arrangement with Random House, Inc.

My Sister Is My Friend by Hannah Markley. From SIGNATURES, EMERGENT READERS: MY SISTER IS MY FRIEND, copyright © 1995 by Harcourt Brace & Company. Reprinted by permission of the publisher.

Pet Day by Lois Bick. From SIGNATURES, INSTANT READERS: PET DAY, Grade 1, copyright © 1996 by Harcourt Brace & Company. Reprinted by permission of the publisher.

Sam's Seasons by Christine Price. Copyright © 1997 by Steck-Vaughn Company.

So Can I by Margery Facklam. Text copyright © 1988 by Margery Facklam. Illustration copyright © 1988 by Jeni Bassett. Reprinted by permission of Harcourt Brace & Company.

From *Soccer Game!* by Grace Maccarone, illustrated by Meredith Johnson. A Hello Reader! Book published by Cartwheel Books, a division of Scholastic Inc. Text copyright © 1994 by Grace Maccarone, illustrations copyright © 1994 by Meredith Johnson. Reprinted by permission of Scholastic Inc. HELLO READER! and CARTWHEEL BOOKS are registered trademarks of Scholastic Inc.

"The Surprise Party" by Mary Cockett. From *Away Went the Hat and Other Stories* by Mary Cockett. Copyright © 1989 by Thomas Nelson & Sons, Ltd. Reprinted by permission of the author.

There Is a Town by Gail Herman. Text copyright © 1996 by Gail Herman. Illustrations copyright © 1996 by Katy Bratun. Reprinted by arrangement with Random House, Inc.

Illustration Credits

Ken Bowser, pp. 4, 5, 34, 35, 70, 96; Jeni Bassett, cover, pp. 6–14; Katy Bratun, pp. 16–22; Jackie Morris, pp. 24–32; Larry Johnson, cover, pp. 36–40; Winifred Barnum-Newman, cover, pp. 50–56; Steve Henry, pp. 58–60, 62–64, 66–68; Meredith Johnson, pp. 72–78; Shirley Bellwood, pp. 81–85; Wallace Keller, cover, pp. 88–94; Lynn Munsinger, pp. 110–120; Nan Brooks, cover, pp. 122–130; Mike Krone, pp. 132–134, 136–138, 140–142.

Photography Credits

Cover Sam Dudgeon; p. 5 Rick Williams; p. 35 Rick Williams; p. 42 © Joe Szkodzinski/Image Bank; p. 43 © John Rich; p. 44 © John Elk/Stock Boston; p. 45 © Susan Van Etten; p. 46 © Park Street; p. 47 © David Hamilton/Image Bank; p. 48a © Joe Szkodzinski/Image Bank; p. 48b © John Rich; p. 48c © John Elk/Stock Boston; p. 48d © Susan Van Etten; p. 48e © Park Street; p. 48f © David Hamilton/Image Bank; p. 71 Rick Williams; p. 97 Rick Williams; pp. 98, 99, 100, 101, 102, 103, 104, 105, 106, 107, 108 © 1990 Fiona Pragoff.